AN INTRODUCTION BY THE GOVERNOR OF ALASKA, SARAH PALIN

Alaska is recognised the world over for its effective resource management practices, producing premium wild and sustainable seafood.

Alaska seafood develops in some of the world's cleanest marine and freshwater habitats. Our long-term fishery management practices ensure that this unmatched, delicious resource can be enjoyed for generations to come.

This book, packed full of delicious recipes, will inspire you to make the most of this wild, wonderful Alaska seafood.

Sarah Palin

Alaska Seafood Marketing Institute

Alaska is an extraordinary and unique land. It is the largest of America's 50 states by a long, long way and yet has one of the smallest populations - over 40% of which live in and around Anchorage! Wild and mostly uninhabited, Alaska has a spectacular natural beauty and is home to an abundance of wildlife and marine life. A wide range of wild fish and shellfish swim freely in Alaska's pristine waters including five species of salmon (King, Sockeye, Coho, Pink and Keta), halibut, pollock, black cod, Pacific cod, whitefish and several varieties of crab (King, Dungeness and Snow). Three million lakes, 3,000

wild ALASKA SEAFOOD

wild ALASKA SEAFOOD

rivers and 34,000 miles of coastline make Alaska one of the most significant fishing areas in the world. It's the only US state to have coastlines on three different seas - the Arctic, the Pacific and the Bering. Alaska is home to abundant stocks of many species of fish, and offers some of the cleanest marine, freshwater, and upland habitats in the world. Effective fisheries' management by federal and state organisations ensures that the fisheries remain productive and sustainable, clean and healthy. Alaska is recognised worldwide as a proven leader in the effective management of natural seafood resources.

WILD ALASKA HALIBUT WITH BROWN BUTTER & CAPERS

Serves 4

75g (3oz) butter
4 x 100-150g (4-6oz) fillets wild Alaska halibut
4 tbsp capers, drained
Freshly ground black pepper

Heat the butter in a large frying pan until melted and bubbling.

Add the halibut fillets and cook them over a medium high heat, spooning the hot butter over them as they cook. They will take about 6 to 8 minutes, depending on the thickness of the fillets. When cooked, the flesh will be opaque and should flake easily when tested with a fork.

Add the capers to the frying pan and cook for a few seconds.

Serve the fish with the hot browned butter sauce spooned over them. Season with a little freshly ground black pepper (it's unlikely that you will need salt, as the capers are salty).

Cook's tip: Serve with lightly cooked green vegetables, such as green beans, sugar snap peas or broccoli and new potatoes. For a change try making this recipe with wild Pacific cod.

SMOKED WILD ALASKA SALMON & PACIFIC COD CHOWDER

Serves 4

25g (1oz) butter
1 onion, finely chopped
1 large leek, thinly sliced
450g (1lb) potatoes, peeled and cut into small chunks
600ml (1pt) vegetable or chicken stock
1 tbsp dill, chopped
1 tbsp parsley, chopped

300g (10oz) wild Pacific cod fillet, skinned and cut into chunks
150g (6oz) smoked wild Alaska salmon, snipped into pieces
2 tbsp cornflour
300ml ($^1/_2$pt) milk
Salt and freshly ground black pepper

Melt the butter in a large saucepan and gently fry the onion and leek over a medium heat for 2 or 3 minutes, until softened, but not browned.

Add the potatoes and stock. Bring up to the boil, then reduce the heat and simmer for about 10 minutes, or until the potatoes are just tender.

Add the herbs to the saucepan with the chunks of cod and smoked salmon. Continue to simmer gently for 3 or 4 minutes.

Blend the cornflour with 2 or 3 tablespoons of the milk, then stir this into the saucepan with the rest of the milk. Heat, stirring gently, until the soup thickens and is piping hot. Season to taste, then ladle into warm bowls.

Cook's tip: Add a handful of frozen peas or sweetcorn (or both) when you add the fish.

WILD ALASKA BLACK COD ON ROSEMARY FOCACCIA

Serves 4

5 tbsp olive oil, plus a little extra
1 large garlic clove, crushed
1 small aubergine, very finely chopped
2 large tomatoes, finely chopped
3 tbsp sun-dried tomato paste
Few drops of balsamic vinegar

Ready-to-bake rosemary focaccia, 4 thick slices
4 x 150g (6oz) fillets wild Alaska black cod, skinned
2 tbsp pine nuts
Salt and freshly ground black pepper

Preheat the oven to 190°C / fan oven 170°C / Gas Mark 5. Grease a shallow baking dish or roasting pan with a few drops of the olive oil.

Heat the remaining olive oil in a large frying pan and add the garlic and aubergine, cooking over a medium-low heat until very soft, about 4 or 5 minutes.

Add the chopped tomatoes and sun-dried tomato paste to the aubergine. Season with a few drops of balsamic vinegar and some salt and pepper to taste. Cook gently for another 2 or 3 minutes.

Spread the slices of focaccia with half the aubergine mixture, and arrange them in the baking dish or roasting pan. Top each one with a black cod fillet, then spoon the remaining aubergine mixture on top. Drizzle a little extra olive oil on top.

Bake for 15-18 minutes, sprinkling the pine nuts on top after the fish has baked for 10 minutes. To check that the fish is cooked, the flesh will be opaque and should flake easily when tested with a fork. Serve, garnished with basil or oregano sprigs.

Cook's tip: As an alternative to black cod, use wild Pacific cod or wild Alaska halibut.

WILD ALASKA CRAB OPEN LASAGNE

Serves 2

250g (9oz) asparagus, trimmed
2 tbsp olive oil
225g (8oz) spinach, washed
3 fresh lasagne sheets, cut in half
25g (1oz) butter
6 spring onions, trimmed and thinly sliced

6 tbsp green pesto sauce
Finely grated zest and juice of 1 small lemon
300g (10oz) wild Alaska crab meat, cooked and flaked
Salt and freshly ground black pepper
3-4 tbsp Parmesan cheese, finely grated

Preheat a char-grill pan or the grill. Brush the asparagus with the olive oil, then char-grill or grill the spears for 6 to 8 minutes, turning often.

Cook the spinach in a tiny amount of water for about 2 minutes, until the leaves have wilted. Drain well, squeezing out the excess moisture with the back of a spoon. At the same time, cook the lasagne for 3 or 4 minutes, or according to pack instructions.

Melt the butter in a frying pan and sauté the spring onions for 2 or 3 minutes, until softened. Stir in the pesto sauce, lemon zest and lemon juice. Heat gently for a few moments, and season to taste.

Drain the lasagne sheets well, and then layer them in two warmed bowls with the pesto mixture, spinach, crab and asparagus. Drizzle any remaining pesto mixture on top, then serve, sprinkled with Parmesan cheese.

Cook's tip: You could use dried lasagne sheets, though you will have to cook them for a few minutes longer and cut them in half once they have cooked.

WILD PACIFIC COD GOUJONS WITH THAI LEMONGRASS DIP

All you do is cut the flesh of two generously sized skinless **wild Pacific cod fillets** into thick strips. Season the fish with **salt and pepper**, then dip in **beaten egg** and roll them in ground **instant polenta** or semolina. Bake at 190°C / fan oven 170°C / Gas Mark 5 for 12-15 minutes, until golden and crunchy. Serve them with a dip made with 4 tbsp **sweet chilli sauce**, 2 tbsp **Thai fish sauce**, 2 tbsp **lime juice**, 1 tbsp very finely **chopped lemongrass** and 2 tbsp chopped **fresh coriander**.

SEARED WILD ALASKA SALMON WITH DILL MAYONNAISE

Just heat 2 or 3 tbsp of olive oil in a large frying pan, then add **skinless wild Alaska salmon fillets** – weighing 125-150g (5-6oz) each. Make sure that you cook them without moving them for the first 2 or 3 minutes, so that they sear and brown. Turn them over to cook the other side for another 2 or 3 minutes, depending on their thickness. Check that they are done – the flesh will be opaque and should flake easily when tested with a fork. Serve with dollops of **good-quality mayonnaise** mixed with 2 or 3 tbsp of chopped **fresh dill**.

SMOKED WILD ALASKA SALMON PLATTER

Simply open some packs of **smoked wild Alaska salmon** and lay the slices out on a platter. Serve with a quick and easy cucumber salad – just peel, halve, deseed and slice half a **cucumber**, then add 1 tsp **caster sugar**, some **salt and peppe**r and enough **white wine vinegar** to cover. Serve with **gherkins, caperberries** or capers – or any other pickles and side dishes that you fancy.

WILD ALASKA POLLOCK, PRAWN & PEA BIRIYANI

For four, cook 225g (8oz) **basmati rice** in lightly salted boiling water for about 12 minutes. Meanwhile, heat 2 tbsp **olive oil** in a large frying pan. Add 1 sliced **onion,** 2 thinly sliced **garlic** cloves and 1 finely chopped **green chilli**. Fry gently for 3 or 4 minutes. Stir in 1 tbsp **medium curry powder**, $1/2$ tsp **cumin seeds** and $1/2$ tsp **ground turmeric**. Add 250g (9oz) **wild Alaska pollock**, cut into pieces, 75g (3oz) cooked peeled **prawns** and 75g (3oz) **frozen peas**. Cook gently, stirring, for 5 or 6 minutes. Drain the rice and add to the frying pan with 12 halved **cherry tomatoes** and 2 tbsp chopped **fresh coriander**. Cook and stir for another 1 or 2 minutes. Season, and then serve.

STEAMED WILD ALASKA SALMON, CHINESE-STYLE

Serves 2

300ml ($^1/_2$ pt) vegetable stock
2 tbsp soy sauce
1 garlic clove, crushed
1 tsp grated fresh root ginger
$^1/_2$ tsp Chinese five-spice powder
4 spring onions, finely sliced

1 small red pepper, deseeded and thinly sliced
2 celery sticks, thinly sliced
Handful of beansprouts
2 heads pak choi, roughly shredded
2 x 100-150g (4-6oz) fillets wild Alaska salmon
Salt and freshly ground black pepper

Pour the vegetable stock into a wok or sauté pan. Add the soy sauce, garlic, ginger, Chinese five-spice powder and all the vegetables. Bring up to simmering point.

Lay the salmon fillets on top of the vegetables and put a lid on top, or cover with a sheet of foil. Cook for 6 to 8 minutes, or until the fish is done. The flesh will be opaque and should flake easily when tested with a fork.

Taste the broth, seasoning with salt and pepper if needed, or add a little more soy sauce. Ladle into warm bowls and serve at once.

Cook's tip: To make the dish more substantial, serve with rice or egg noodles.

SIMPLE WILD ALASKA SEAFOOD PAELLA

Serves 4

Generous pinch of saffron strands
2 tbsp olive oil
1 bunch spring onions, trimmed and chopped
1 garlic clove, crushed
225g (8oz) Spanish paella rice or risotto rice
1 red pepper, deseeded and chopped
900ml (1 1/2 pt) fish or vegetable stock
100g (4oz) frozen petit pois or garden peas, thawed

225g (8oz) wild Alaska salmon fillet, skinned and cut into chunks
225g (8oz) wild Alaska pollock, halibut or Pacific cod fillet, skinned and cut into chunks
100g (4oz) wild Alaska crab, cut into chunks
100g (4oz) cooked peeled prawns, thawed if frozen
2 tbsp fresh parsley, chopped
Salt and freshly ground black pepper

Put the saffron stands into a small bowl and add 3 tablespoons boiling water. Leave to infuse for about 10 minutes.

Meanwhile, heat the oil in a large sauté pan or non-stick frying pan and gently fry the spring onions and garlic until softened, but not brown.

Add the rice and red pepper to the pan with the saffron and its soaking liquid. Stir in the stock. Bring to the boil, then reduce the heat and simmer for 15-20 minutes, stirring often, until most of the liquid has been absorbed.

Add the petit pois or garden peas, salmon, white fish and crab. Cook gently, stirring occasionally, for 5 minutes, and then add the prawns and parsley. Stir them through and cook for another 1 or 2 minutes to heat thoroughly. Season to taste, then serve.

Cook's tip: Look out for Spanish paella rice or select good quality risotto rice.

WILD ALASKA POLLOCK GRATIN

Serves 4

500g (1lb 2oz) wild Alaska pollock fillet,
thawed if frozen
450ml (¾ pt) milk
40g (1½ oz) butter
40g (1½ oz) plain flour
100g (4oz) mature Cheddar, grated

1 tsp wholegrain mustard
50g (2oz) fresh breadcrumbs
A few tiny sprigs of fresh rosemary,
plus extra to garnish
Salt and freshly ground black pepper

Preheat a medium grill. Put four individual gratin dishes, or one large shallow baking dish in the grill compartment to warm.

Put the fish fillets into a large frying pan and cover with water. Heat and simmer gently for 5 or 6 minutes, or until the fish is just cooked. (The flesh should flake easily when tested with a fork). Drain thoroughly, and share the fish between the warm dishes.

To make the sauce, put the milk, butter and flour into a non-stick saucepan, all at once. Heat, stirring constantly with a small whisk, until the sauce thickens. Remove from the heat and add about three-quarters of the cheese, stirring until melted. Add the mustard, then season to taste.

Share the sauce between the gratin dishes, pouring it over the fish. Scatter the breadcrumbs, rosemary sprigs and remaining cheese over the top. Grill for 3 or 4 minutes, until browned and bubbling. Serve at once, garnished with extra rosemary.

Cook's tip: Another time use wild Alaska halibut or Pacific cod instead of pollock.

ROAST WILD PACIFIC COD ON PUY LENTILS

Serves 2

300g (10oz) butternut squash, cut into 2cm (3/4 inch) cubes
2 carrots, sliced
1 red onion, sliced into wedges
1 leek, sliced
2 tbsp olive oil
Salt and freshly ground black pepper

150g (6oz) puy lentils, rinsed and drained
2 tsp vegetable stock powder (or 1/2 vegetable stock cube)
100g (4oz) sun-blush tomatoes in olive oil, roughly chopped
2 x 100-150g (4-6oz) fillets wild Pacific cod, skinned

Preheat the oven to 200°C / fan oven 180°C / Gas Mark 6.

Put the butternut squash, carrots, red onion and leek into a roasting pan. Add the olive oil, season with salt and pepper and toss together. Roast in the oven for 25-30 minutes, until the vegetables are tender.

Meanwhile, put the lentils into a saucepan and cover them with twice their volume of water. Add the stock powder or cube, bring up to the boil, then reduce the heat and simmer, uncovered, for 15-20 minutes, until tender. Drain well.

Add the lentils and sun-blush tomatoes to the roasted vegetables, stirring them through gently. Arrange the cod fillets on top and drizzle them with a little olive oil (use oil from the jar of sun-blush tomatoes to give them extra flavour). Cover the roasting pan with a piece of foil and return to the oven to bake for a further 12-15 minutes, or until the fish is cooked. The flesh will be opaque and should flake easily when tested with a fork. Serve.

Cook's tips: Serve with a dressed green salad and fresh, crusty bread. You can prepare ahead to the point where the fish is arranged on top - then just cover with foil and refrigerate. Remember to cook for a little longer to ensure that everything is piping hot.

sustainable

All Alaska seafood is wild and sustainable. Since 1959, Alaska's constitution has mandated that 'Fish . . . be utilized, developed and maintained on the sustained yield principle'. This long-term dedication to sustainability has ensured continuous, wild and healthy harvests and that Alaska's stocks of superior seafood are preserved for future generations. Unlike many of the world's fisheries, Alaska's are managed for protection against overfishing, habitat damage and pollution. In Alaska, protecting the future of both fish stocks and the environment takes priority over opportunities for commercial harvest. Alaska's exemplary fisheries' management practices are characterised by the unusual degree of collaboration among the state, federal and

sustainable

international organisations that are charged with protecting this valuable resource. In fact, no Alaska seafood is classified as overfished. As a result of effective management, Alaska's salmon harvests have increased well beyond historical levels.

Alaska's fisheries are globally recognised as a model of sustainability. In addition, significant bycatch reduction programmes are enforced in all Alaska's fisheries. Entire communities have been intimately involved with the harvesting and processing of

Alaska's commercial catch for generations. Thousands of families continue to make their living from the resources of Alaska's rugged coastline, and fishing and seafood processing employ more people than any other industry in Alaska.

wild ALASKA SEAFOOD **29**

SMOKED WILD ALASKA SALMON PASTA WITH GOAT'S CHEESE

Serves 4

200g (7oz) smoked wild Alaska salmon
400g (14oz) pasta shells
4 tbsp olive oil
1 garlic clove, crushed

50g (2oz) pine nuts
8-10 sage leaves, torn into pieces
200g (7oz) goat's cheese, broken onto pieces
Salt and freshly ground black pepper

Snip or tear the salmon into pieces.

Cook the pasta in a large saucepan of lightly salted boiling water for 8 to 10 minutes, or according to pack instructions, until tender.

Meanwhile, heat the olive oil in a frying pan and gently fry the garlic and pine nuts until lightly browned for about 1 or 2 minutes. Remove from the heat and add the torn sage leaves.

Drain the cooked pasta and return it to the saucepan, adding the smoked salmon, olive oil, garlic, pine nuts and sage. Season with salt and freshly ground black pepper to taste. Add the goat's cheese, and then stir the ingredients together gently.

Share the pasta between four warm plates or bowls. Serve at once.

Cook's tip: For a bit of a kick, fry one small, deseeded and finely chopped red chilli with the garlic and pine nuts.

WILD ALASKA BLACK COD WITH SAFFRON RISOTTO

Serves 4

Generous pinch of saffron strands
900ml (1 1/2 pt) hot vegetable stock
2 tbsp olive oil
225g (8oz) risotto rice
4 spring onions, trimmed and chopped
1 garlic clove, crushed
150ml (1/4 pt) dry white wine
4 x 150g (6oz) fillets wild Alaska black cod

150ml (1/4 pt) milk
1 bay leaf
4 tbsp Parmesan cheese, finely grated
75g (3oz) frozen petit pois or garden peas, thawed
Salt and freshly ground black pepper
Basil leaves, to garnish

Add the saffron stands to the hot vegetable stock and leave to infuse while starting to cook the risotto.

Heat the oil in a large sauté pan or non-stick frying pan for a few moments, and add the rice. Cook over a low heat for about 2 minutes, stirring, until the rice looks shiny, but not brown.

Add the spring onions and garlic, then pour in the white wine and let it bubble up for a few moments. Add a couple of ladlefuls of stock. Stir, then cook over a medium heat for 20-25 minutes, gradually adding the remaining stock, until the rice is tender and creamy.

About 10 minutes before the risotto is ready, start to cook the fish. Put the fillets into a shallow pan with a lid and add the milk, bay leaf and 150ml (1/4 pint) boiling water. Season lightly. Cover and simmer gently for 6 to 8 minutes, or until the fish flakes easily when tested with a fork.

Add the Parmesan and peas to the risotto, stirring them through gently. Season with salt and pepper to taste. Serve the risotto with the fish, garnished with basil leaves.

Cook's tip: For a deliciously creamy risotto choose Italian arborio or carnaroli rice. If you can't find black cod try substituting with wild Pacific cod.

WILD ALASKA SALMON EN CROUTE

Serves 2

Vegetable oil, for greasing
300g (10oz) spinach, washed
250g (9oz) ready-to-use puff pastry,
thawed if frozen
2 x 100-150g (4-6oz) fillets wild Alaska salmon,
skinned

2 tsp green or red pesto sauce
Salt and freshly ground black pepper
Beaten egg, to glaze

Preheat the oven to 220°C / fan oven 200°C / Gas Mark 7. Brush a baking sheet with a little vegetable oil.

Pack the spinach into a large saucepan and cook it, without adding any extra water, until the leaves wilt - this will take about 3 or 4 minutes. (There will be enough water on the spinach from washing it). Cool, then drain well, squeezing out the excess moisture with your hands.

Cut the pastry into two equal pieces. Roll them out on a lightly floured surface into 18cm (7inch) squares, trimming the edges with a sharp knife. Place a rectangular pile of spinach in the middle of each square and sit a salmon fillet on top. Spread 1 teaspoon of pesto sauce over the surface of each piece of fish, and season with a little salt and pepper to taste. Brush the pastry edges with beaten egg, fold up around each salmon fillet and press the edges together firmly to seal them. Brush the pastry with beaten egg, to glaze. Place on the prepared baking sheet.

Bake for 18-20 minutes until well-risen and golden brown. Serve with fresh vegetables or salad.

Cook's tip: Get ahead earlier in the day by preparing up to the point where the salmon en croute are baked. Keep covered and refrigerated until you are ready to cook.

GRILLED WILD ALASKA HALIBUT WITH LEMON & THYME DRESSING

Serves 4

4 x 100-150g (4-6oz) fillets wild Alaska halibut
75g (3oz) butter
Finely grated zest and juice of 1 large lemon
2 tsp Dijon mustard
4 sprigs lemon thyme
2 tbsp olive oil

2 leeks, sliced
2 courgettes, sliced
225g (8oz) baby spinach leaves
2 tbsp dry white wine or vegetable stock
Salt and freshly ground black pepper

Preheat the grill. Arrange the halibut fillets on the grill rack, placing a knob of butter on top of each one. Sprinkle them with a few drops of lemon juice, then season with a little salt and pepper. Grill for 6 to 8 minutes, depending on the thickness of the fillets.

While the fish is cooking, put the rest of the butter into a saucepan with the lemon zest, remaining lemon juice and mustard. Heat gently, whisking until melted, then add the thyme sprigs. Keep warm over a low heat.

Heat the olive oil in a wok or large frying pan and sauté the leeks and courgettes for 4 or 5 minutes. Add the spinach and wine or stock, stirring until the leaves have wilted - about 1 minute.

Serve the fish and vegetables, pouring a little warm lemon and thyme dressing over each one.

Cook's tip: Use regular thyme if you can't find the lemon variety, or use rosemary instead.

WILD PACIFIC COD WITH TOMATO, MOZZARELLA & BASIL

Simply mix 3 tbsp **sun-dried tomato paste** with 25g (1oz) chopped **pitted olives**. Place 4 x 125-150g (5-6oz) fillets of **wild Pacific cod** on a baking sheet greased with a little **olive oil**. Spread the tomato mixture onto the fillets, and arrange thin slices of **mozzarella cheese** over them. Top with little bunches of **cherry tomatoes** on the vine, and drizzle with a little more olive oil. Roast for 12-15 minutes at 190°C / fan oven 170°C / Gas Mark 5, then serve, garnished with **basil leaves**.

WILD ALASKA HALIBUT WITH LEMON & PRAWN

Take 4 x 125-150g (5-6oz) fillets of **wild Alaska halibut** and arrange them in a roasting tin greased with **olive oil**. Mix together 100g (4oz) **fresh breadcrumbs**, 40g (1$^{1}/_{2}$ oz) melted **butter** and the finely grated **zest and juice of a lemon**. Stir in 100g (4oz) cooked peeled **prawns** and 2 tbsp chopped **fresh parsley**. Season with **salt and pepper** and spread the topping over the fillets. Roast for 12-15 minutes at 190°C / fan oven 170°C / Gas Mark 5.

WILD ALASKA SALMON WITH HORSERADISH, WALNUTS & HERBS

For two people, take 2 x 125-150g (5-6oz) fillets of **wild Alaska salmon** and arrange them in a roasting pan, greased with a little olive oil. In a mixing bowl, combine 3 tbsp **horseradish sauce**, 5 tbsp finely **chopped walnuts** and 1 tbsp each of chopped **fresh chives, parsley and tarragon**. Mix in 15g ($^{1}/_{2}$ oz) softened **butter** and a little **salt and pepper**. Spread evenly over the salmon fillets, then roast for 12-15 minutes at 190°C / fan oven 170°C / Gas Mark 5.

WILD ALASKA SALMON WITH ORANGE & WATERCRESS

Melt a knob of **butter** in a roasting pan with a splash of **olive oil**. Heat for a moment, and add a couple of 125g-150g (5-6oz) **wild Alaska salmon** fillets. Transfer to the oven, pre-heated to 190°C / fan oven 170°C / Gas Mark 5. Roast for 8 to 10 minutes. While the fish is cooking, roughly chop a handful of **watercress** and add 3 tbsp finely chopped **cucumber**. Using a sharp, serrated knife, remove all the peel and pith from 1 small **orange**. Cut into segments, removing all the membrane, then mix with the cucumber and watercress. Season with a few drops of **wine vinegar, salt and pepper**, and serve with the fish.

Cook's tip: These topping ideas are interchangeable - just choose your favourite fish and try it with one of the four suggestions.

WARM WILD ALASKA SALMON NIÇOISE

Serves 4

500g (1lb 2oz) new potatoes, scrubbed
4 eggs
4 x 150g (6oz) fillets wild Alaska salmon
25g (1oz) butter
150g (6oz) fine green beans, trimmed
6 tbsp olive oil
1 tsp Dijon mustard
3 tbsp lemon juice

Salt and freshly ground black pepper
1 Romaine or cos lettuce, roughly shredded
4 tomatoes, quartered
100g (4oz) black or green olives
25g (1oz) anchovy fillets in olive oil, drained
2 tbsp capers
Plenty of flat leaf parsley, chopped

Cook the potatoes in lightly salted simmering water for 20 minutes, or until tender. At the same time, cook the eggs in boiling water for 12 minutes, covering them with cold water when cooked.

Preheat the grill. Arrange the salmon fillets on the grill rack and place a small knob of butter on top of each one. Grill the salmon for about 6 to 8 minutes, depending on the thickness of the fillets. Set to one side while making the salad.

Lightly cook the green beans in boiling water for 4 or 5 minutes - they need to remain quite crunchy. Drain them well.

Make the dressing by whisking together the olive oil, mustard and lemon juice. Season with a little salt and black pepper to taste. Drain the potatoes thoroughly and add them to the dressing while hot - this means that they will absorb the flavour of the dressing as they cool.

Share the lettuce, cooled potatoes, tomatoes, green beans and olives between four serving plates or bowls. Shell the eggs, quarter them and place them on the salads. Arrange the salmon fillets with the anchovies placed on top. Drizzle with any remaining dressing and scatter the capers and parsley over the salads. Serve at once.

Cook's tip: If you cook the potatoes and eggs in advance, it will only take you about 10 minutes to put these delicious salads together.

wild ALASKA SEAFOOD

WILD ALASKA POLLOCK CURRY

Serves 4

400g (14oz) wild Alaska pollock fillet, thawed if frozen
3 tbsp olive oil
1 onion, chopped
2 garlic cloves, crushed
1 tsp cumin seeds
1 tsp ground coriander
1 tbsp Korma or mild curry powder
1 courgette, sliced
1 carrot, chopped into chunks

1 aubergine, chopped into chunks
1 red pepper, deseeded and chopped into chunks
2 x 400g cans chopped tomatoes
450ml (³/₄ pt) vegetable or chicken stock
1 x 400g can chick peas, drained
50g (2oz) red lentils
2 tbsp coriander, chopped
Salt and freshly ground black pepper
Naan bread or rice, to serve

Pat the wild Alaska pollock fillets dry with kitchen paper and then cut them into large chunks.

Heat the olive oil in a large saucepan. Gently fry the onion and garlic for 2 or 3 minutes, until softened. Stir in the cumin seeds, ground coriander and curry powder and stir for a few seconds.

Add the courgette, carrot, aubergine, pepper and canned tomatoes. Pour in the stock and add the chick peas and lentils. Bring to the boil, then reduce the heat and simmer for 20-30 minutes, or until the vegetables are tender and the lentils are soft.

Add the pollock chunks to the saucepan, stirring them in gently. Simmer the curry for a further 5 minutes to cook the fish. Stir in the fresh coriander and season, adding salt and pepper, to taste.

Ladle into warm bowls and serve with hot naan bread or rice.

Cook's tip: It's important that you serve the curry soon after adding the pollock, otherwise the fish will break up into small flakes. If you wish to make the curry in advance, add the fish when you re-heat the curry, simmering it for 4 or 5 minutes.

WILD PACIFIC COD WITH CAULIFLOWER, BACON AND SPINACH

Serves 2

300g (10oz) wild Pacific cod fillet, skinned and cut into chunks
Finely grated zest and juice of 1 small lemon
300g (10oz) cauliflower, broken into florets
75g (3oz) bacon lardons or streaky bacon, chopped

15g ($^{1}/_{2}$ oz) butter
$^{1}/_{2}$ tsp cumin seeds
Pinch chilli flakes
2 tbsp croutons
Salt and freshly ground black pepper
2 generous handfuls baby spinach leaves

Put the chunks of fish into a non-metallic bowl and add the lemon zest and juice, tossing to coat. Leave them to marinate for 5 to 8 minutes, and drain off the lemon juice. Meanwhile, cook the cauliflower for 5 to 8 minutes in lightly salted boiling water, until just tender (take care that it doesn't overcook). Drain well.

Heat a large non-stick frying pan or wok and add the bacon lardons or streaky bacon, cooking them until crisp. Remove them from the pan with a slotted spoon and set to one side.

Melt the butter in the frying pan or wok, and then add the cauliflower, cumin seeds and chilli flakes. Stir-fry for 2 or 3 minutes over a medium-high heat, then add the chunks of fish and cook for a further 2 minutes.

Return the bacon to the pan and add the croutons. Cook and stir for a few moments, season with a little salt and freshly ground black pepper, then serve with the spinach tossed through.

Cook's tip: Stir the ingredients together gently so that you don't break up the chunks of fish. For a change try this recipe with wild Alaska halibut instead of Pacific cod.

WILD ALASKA SALMON AND SPINACH ROULADE

Serves 4 as a main course, 8 as a starter

Vegetable oil, for greasing
225g (8oz) wild Alaska salmon fillet, skinned
300g (10oz) fresh spinach, thoroughly washed
4 eggs, separated
50g (2oz) Parmesan cheese, finely grated
200g tub low fat soft cheese

4 tbsp crème fraiche
2 tomatoes, deseeded and chopped
2 tbsp fresh herbs, chopped (chives, parsley or dill)
Salt and freshly ground black pepper

Preheat the oven to 200°C / fan oven 180°C / Gas Mark 6. Grease and line a 20 x 30cm (8 x 12 inch) Swiss roll tin with non-stick baking paper. Grease with a little vegetable oil.

Place the salmon fillet onto a lightly greased baking sheet and cover with a piece of foil. Set aside.

Cook the spinach in a small amount of water for about 5 minutes, until wilted. Drain thoroughly, squeezing out the excess moisture, and then chop finely. Cool. Tip into a large bowl and mix in the egg yolks. Stir in the grated cheese and season with salt and pepper.

In a large, grease-free bowl, whisk the egg whites until they hold their shape. Fold into the spinach mixture, using a large metal spoon. Pour into prepared tin and spread into the corners. Bake for 10-12 minutes until set and light golden brown. At the same time, bake the salmon for 8 to 10 minutes.

Turn out the roulade onto a large sheet of greaseproof paper. Peel away the lining and leave to cool. Let the salmon cool, then flake it with a fork.

Beat the low fat soft cheese until smooth and creamy, then mix in the crème fraiche, flaked salmon, tomatoes and herbs. Season. Spread over the roulade, and roll up from the short end. Chill until ready to serve.

Cook's tip: Make sure you use a very sharp knife for slicing the roulade neatly.

WILD ALASKA SALMON & HALIBUT PIE

Serves 4

25g (1oz) butter
700g (1¹/₂ lb) potatoes, peeled
150g (6oz) courgettes, sliced
350g (12oz) wild Alaska halibut fillet, skinned
350g (12oz) wild Alaska salmon fillet, skinned
200ml (¹/₃ pt) vegetable stock
1 bay leaf
200ml (¹/₃ pt) dry white wine

2 tbsp cornflour, blended with 3 tbsp single cream or milk
75g (3oz) frozen petit pois or garden peas, thawed
1 tbsp dill, chopped
3-4 tbsp milk
Salt and freshly ground black pepper

Preheat the oven to 190°C / fan oven 170°C / Gas Mark 5. Grease a baking dish with a small knob of butter.

Cook the potatoes in lightly salted boiling water for about 20 minutes, until tender. At the same time, cook the courgettes for about 5 minutes, then drain them well.

Meanwhile, put the fish fillets into a shallow pan with the stock, bay leaf and another knob of butter. Heat and simmer gently, partially covered, for 5 or 6 minutes, until the fish is cooked. The flesh will be opaque and should flake easily when tested with a fork. Use a draining spoon to lift the fish into the baking dish.

Pour the white wine into the pan with the fish cooking liquid. Remove the bay leaf. Add the blended cornflour and heat, stirring constantly, until thickened and smooth. Stir in the peas, courgettes and dill. Season, and then pour into the baking dish, gently combining it with the fish.

Drain the potatoes and mash them with the milk and any remaining butter. Season with a little salt and pepper to taste. Spoon on top of the fish mixture, spreading it out to cover the entire surface. If you prefer, pipe the potato on top of the fish. Transfer to the oven and bake for 25-30 minutes, until the potato topping is golden brown.

Cook's tip: Place the fish pie under a hot grill for the final few minutes to make sure that the topping is well browned.

Alaska is one of the few remaining wildernesses on earth. It is by far the largest of America's 50 states and yet this vast and magnificent land remains largely uninhabited. Alaska's dramatic snow capped mountains, glaciers, forests, green plains, clear and clean waters provide ideal and unspoilt habitats for a huge variety of marine life and wildlife. The spectacular Alaskan landscape with its miles and miles of uninhabited wilderness is home to an abundance of wildlife including black and grizzly bears, moose, and bald eagles. Magnificent humpback and killer whales, and a wealth of Alaska fish and shellfish live

wild ALASKA SEAFOOD

wild

in its seas. Alaska seafood swims wild in the exceptionally clean and icy waters feeding on natural foods in the Gulf of Alaska, and develops a firm texture and delicious flavour. Their diet of crustaceans and other marine life give wild Alaska salmon, in particular, its distinctive colour and taste. Alaska's whales, sea lions, otters and birds are carefully protected, and hundreds of square miles of sensitive habitat have been protected as Marine Protected Areas (MPAs). More than 40 Marine Protected Areas have been established in the waters off Alaska to safeguard them from human activity.

wild ALASKA SEAFOOD   53

WILD ALASKA SALMON & POLLOCK FISH CAKES

Serves 4

900g (2lb) potatoes, peeled and cut into large chunks
Pinch of salt
200g (7oz) wild Alaska salmon fillet
150g (6oz) wild Alaska pollock fillet
2 hard-boiled eggs, shelled and chopped
4 spring onions, very finely chopped
25g (1oz) gherkins, chopped

2 tbsp capers, drained
2 tbsp parsley, chopped
Freshly ground black pepper
25g (1oz) plain flour
1 small egg, beaten with 2 tbsp cold water
100g (4oz) dried breadcrumbs
Vegetable oil, for frying

Cook the potatoes in lightly salted boiling water for about 20 minutes, until tender. Drain well and mash thoroughly.

Meanwhile, poach the fish fillets in a large frying pan in simmering water for about 6 to 8 minutes. Lift from the pan with a draining spoon. Remove the skin and any bones, then flake the fish into large chunks with a fork.

Mix together the mashed potatoes, salmon, pollock, hard-boiled eggs, spring onions, gherkins, capers and parsley. Season with a little salt and plenty of black pepper, and then form the mixture into eight fish cakes.

Dust each fish cake with a little flour, dip into beaten egg and coat with the breadcrumbs. Cover and chill until ready to cook.

Heat some vegetable oil in a frying pan and gently cook the fish cakes in batches for 4 or 5 minutes on each side.

Cook's tip: Use soaked bulghar wheat or couscous for coating the fish cakes instead of breadcrumbs.

SEARED WILD ALASKA HALIBUT WITH PANCETTA SALAD

Serves 4

4 peppers, halved and deseeded
170g pack pancetta cubes
15g ($^1/_2$ oz) butter
2 tbsp olive oil
4 x 100-150g (4-6oz) fillets wild Alaska halibut
4 handfuls baby spinach
$^1/_2$ red onion, thinly sliced
1 handful pea shoots, rocket or watercress

Dressing:

4 tbsp extra virgin olive oil
2 tbsp lemon juice
$^1/_2$ tsp finely grated lemon zest
1 tsp whole grain or Dijon mustard
2 tsp chopped fresh thyme
Salt and freshly ground black pepper

Preheat the grill. Arrange the peppers on the grill rack cut side down. Grill them under a high heat until the skins begin to blacken and char. Put them on to a plate and cover tightly with cling film or put them into a sealed polythene bag - the steamy atmosphere will help to loosen their skins.

Next, make the dressing by whisking together the olive oil, lemon juice, lemon zest, mustard and seasoning. Set to one side.

Heat a frying pan and add the pancetta cubes, sizzling them until golden brown and crispy. Tip them onto some kitchen paper to drain.

Add the butter and olive oil to the frying pan and heat for a few moments, and then add the halibut fillets. Cook them for about 6 to 8 minutes, turning them to cook on both sides. The flesh will be opaque and should flake easily when tested with a fork, though make sure that you don't overcook the fish.

Place a handful of spinach leaves onto each of four serving plates. Peel the peppers, then tear them into strips and share them between the salads, along with the pancetta and red onion, pea shoots, rocket or watercress.

Serve the halibut with the salads, and drizzle the dressing over them. Serve at once.

Cook's tips: Choose a variety of peppers for colour and flavour, or use ready-roasted peppers in olive oil for speed. Substitute six rashers of smoked streaky bacon for the pancetta, if you prefer.

BEER-BATTERED WILD PACIFIC COD & CHIPS

Serves 4

900g (2lbs) large potatoes, each cut into 8 wedges
2 tbsp olive oil
125g (5oz) plain flour, plus a little extra
$1/2$ tsp salt
1 egg
150ml ($1/4$ pt) light ale
4 x 200-225g (7-8oz) fillets wild Pacific cod

Vegetable oil, for frying
4 tbsp mayonnaise
4 tbsp Greek-style natural yoghurt
25g (1oz) gherkins, finely chopped
2 tbsp capers, chopped
1 tbsp parsley or chives, chopped
Freshly ground black pepper

Preheat the oven to 200°C / fan oven 180°C / Gas Mark 6.

Tip the potato wedges into a large roasting pan and add the olive oil. Season with salt and pepper and toss together. Roast in the oven for 35-40 minutes until browned and crisp, turning once after 20 minutes.

Meanwhile, sift the flour and salt into a large bowl. Add the egg and beer, beating with a wire whisk to make a smooth batter.

Heat the vegetable oil in a wok or large, deep saucepan. Dust the wild Pacific cod fillets with a little flour, and dip them into the batter. Cooking one or two fillets at a time, deep-fry them for 5 or 6 minutes until crisp and cooked. Drain on sheets of kitchen paper.

Make the tartare sauce by mixing together the mayonnaise, yoghurt, gherkins, capers and herbs. Season with black pepper. Serve with the fish and chips.

Cook's tip: For a short cut, use ready-prepared tartare sauce. Wild Alaska pollock is also perfect for this recipe instead of Pacific cod.

WILD ALASKA HALIBUT WITH TARRAGON BEURRE BLANC & SAMPHIRE

Serves 4

25g (1oz) butter
1 tbsp olive oil
4 x 150-200g (6-7oz) fillets wild Alaska halibut
300g (10oz) samphire or asparagus

For the tarragon beurre blanc:
2 shallots or 1 very small onion, very finely chopped
2 tbsp white wine vinegar
4 tbsp dry white wine
2 tbsp double cream
150g (6oz) chilled unsalted butter, diced
1 tbsp tarragon, chopped
Salt and ground white pepper

Heat the butter and olive oil in a large frying pan and add the halibut cheeks or fillets. Cook over a medium-low heat for about 8 minutes, turning once.

Meanwhile, start to make the sauce. Put the shallots or onion into a small saucepan with the wine vinegar, white wine and 6 tablespoons cold water. Bring to the boil, then simmer until almost all of the liquid has evaporated.

While the liquid is reducing, put the samphire or asparagus on to cook in simmering water - only add a pinch of salt to the asparagus, as the samphire is salty enough. It will take 3 or 4 minutes to cook.

Stir the cream into the shallot or onion mixture and cook gently for a few moments, then remove from the heat and whisk in the butter, a little at a time, to give a smooth sauce. Add the chopped tarragon and season with a little salt and pepper to taste.

Serve the halibut with the samphire or asparagus, along with the tarragon beurre blanc.

Cook's tip: Use wild Alaska salmon or Pacific cod instead - with or without the tarragon in the sauce. If you can't find samphire, substitute with asparagus.

SMOKED WILD ALASKA SALMON WRAP WITH HORSERADISH

Give your wraps a bit of a kick with more than a hint of horseradish (it goes brilliantly with smoked salmon). Simply mix 2 or 3 tbsp of low fat **soft cheese** with 2 tsp of **horseradish sauce**. Spread this over a wrap, then top with smoked wild **Alaska salmon, watercress, sliced radish** and **cucumber**. Roll up tightly, slice in half, and eat.

POACHED WILD ALASKA SALMON DELUXE BAGEL

First choose your **bagel** - be it plain, sesame or multi-seed. Split it in two and toast the cut sides lightly, then spread with a little **butter**. Pack full with **rocket**, poached **wild Alaska salmon** and sliced **tomato**, then spoon a little **wholegrain mustard** and **mayonnaise** on top. Sandwich the two halves together and serve at once. Be generous and share it with a friend!

SMOKED WILD ALASKA SALMON WITH LEMON MASCARPONE

Take a couple of generous slices of **farmhouse or granary bread**, spread with a little **butter**, then top one piece with slices of **smoked wild Alaska salmon**. Season with freshly ground **black pepper**. Next, take 2 or 3 tbsp of **mascarpone cheese** and mix in a little finely grated **lemon zest** with a good squeeze of **lemon juice**. Spread over the other slice of bread and sandwich together. Add **cucumber, lettuce or watercress** too, if desired.

SMOKED WILD ALASKA SALMON ITALIAN-STYLE CIABATTA

Take slices of **ciabatta bread**, split them in half and brush them with **olive oil**. Next, heat a char-grill pan or heavy-based frying pan and add the slices of bread, cut sides down, cooking them until lightly charred. Remove and top with **baby spinach leaves, roasted red peppers** (either freshly cooked or from a jar) and slices of **smoked wild Alaska salmon**.

WILD ALASKA FISH STEW, MEDITERRANEAN-STYLE

Serves 4

4 tbsp olive oil
1 onion, chopped
1 large garlic clove, crushed
1 courgette, chopped
1 carrot, chopped
600ml (1pt) tomato passata
1 tbsp fresh oregano, chopped (or 1 tsp dried)
1 tbsp parsley, chopped
300ml (1/2 pt) vegetable stock

150g (6oz) wild Alaska salmon fillet, skinned
150g (6oz) wild Alaska pollock fillet,
thawed if frozen
300g (10oz) mussels, scrubbed
150g (6oz) cooked peeled prawns,
thawed if frozen
Salt and freshly ground black pepper
Fresh oregano or parsley, chopped to garnish

Heat the olive oil in a large saucepan and gently fry the onion, garlic, courgette and carrot for 3 or 4 minutes, without browning.

Add the passata, herbs and stock. Bring to the boil, then reduce the heat and simmer for 10 minutes, or until the carrots are tender.

Add the wild Alaska salmon and pollock to the saucepan in whole fillets - they will break up once they are cooked. Cover and simmer gently for 3 or 4 minutes, then add the mussels, discarding any that are damaged or remain open when tapped. Put the lid on the saucepan and cook for 2 or 3 minutes, until the mussels have opened (discard any that remain shut). Add the prawns and gently stir them through so that you avoid breaking up the fish too much.

Season to taste, then ladle into warm bowls. Serve, garnished with the fresh oregano or parsley.

Cook's tip: For a spicy kick, add a large, finely chopped fresh red chilli with the onion and garlic.

POACHED WILD ALASKA SALMON, PRAWN & AVOCADO SALAD

Serves 4

500g (1lb 2oz) wild Alaska salmon fillet
100g (4oz) rocket
1 bulb fennel, trimmed and thinly sliced
1 bunch spring onions, trimmed and thinly sliced
20 cherry tomatoes, halved
1 avocado, peeled, pitted and sliced

350g (12oz) large cooked peeled prawns,
thawed if frozen
2 tbsp lemon juice
Salt and freshly ground black pepper
4 tbsp mayonnaise
2 tbsp green pesto sauce

Preheat the grill. Arrange the salmon fillets on the grill rack and cook for 6 to 8 minutes, or until the flesh is opaque and flakes easily. Set to one side to cool.

In a large salad bowl, mix together the rocket, fennel, spring onions, cherry tomatoes, avocado and prawns. Break up the salmon into large chunks, removing any skin, and add to the mixture. Share between four serving plates or bowls and sprinkle the lemon juice on top. Season with a little salt and pepper to taste.

Mix the mayonnaise and pesto sauce together and serve with the salad.

Cook's tip: Use mixed salad leaves, watercress or spinach instead of the rocket for a slightly different taste.

WILD PACIFIC COD WITH LIME, HERB & PARMESAN CRUST

Serves 4

4 tbsp olive oil
4 x 100-150g (4-6oz) fillets wild Pacific cod
Finely grated zest and juice of 1 lime
50g (2oz) fresh white breadcrumbs

1 tbsp fresh dill, oregano or parsley, chopped
50g (2oz) Parmesan cheese, finely grated
Salt and freshly ground black pepper
4 thin slices of lime

Preheat the oven to 200°C / fan oven 180°C / Gas Mark 6.

Grease a baking sheet with a few drops of the olive oil, and arrange the fillets of fish on top. Sprinkle them with the lime juice.

Mix together the lime zest, breadcrumbs, herbs, most of the grated cheese and remaining olive oil. Season with a little salt and black pepper. Share between the fish fillets, spreading it over the surface of each one. Sprinkle the reserved Parmesan cheese on top, and then add the lime slices.

Transfer to the oven and bake for 12-15 minutes, or until the fish is opaque and flakes easily when tested with a fork. Serve with lightly cooked fresh vegetables.

Cook's tip: You could easily substitute wild Alaska pollock fillets, halibut or salmon for the cod - the topping works well on all of them.

WILD ALASKA HALIBUT SEVICHE

Serves 4

300g (10oz) wild Alaska halibut fillet, thinly sliced
Finely grated zest of 1 lime
2 limes, juiced
2 tbsp olive oil
1 small red onion, thinly sliced

1 Ramiro red pepper, deseeded and thinly sliced
1 green chilli, deseeded and thinly sliced
2-3 tbsp fresh coriander, chopped
Salt and freshly ground black pepper

Put the slices of halibut into a shallow non-metallic bowl. Add the lime zest and juice, tossing to coat. Cover and leave to marinate for 10 minutes.

Add the olive oil, red onion, pepper and chilli to the fish, tossing to coat. Cover and leave to marinate for a further 10-15 minutes.

Serve, sprinkled with fresh coriander and seasoned with a little salt and plenty of black pepper.

Cook's tip: Another time, make this dish with thinly sliced wild Alaska salmon instead of halibut.

BAKED WILD ALASKA SALMON PARCELS

Serves 4

4 x 125-150g (5-6oz) fillets wild Alaska salmon
1 leek, finely sliced
1 carrot, cut into fine strips
1 bulb fennel, finely sliced
4 small knobs butter

4 slices lemon
4 tbsp dry white wine
Freshly ground black pepper
Dill sprigs, to garnish

Preheat the oven to 200°C / fan oven 180°C / Gas Mark 6. Cut out 4 x 30cm (12 inch) squares of baking parchment or foil.

Place a salmon fillet onto the centre of each piece of parchment or foil. Mix the vegetables together, and share them between the parcels. Top each one with a knob of butter, a slice of lemon and 1 tablespoon of wine. Season with black pepper.

Fold the paper or foil over the fish and vegetables, scrunching it up to seal tightly. Place on baking sheets and bake for 12-15 minutes.

Unwrap the parcels and serve, garnished with dill sprigs.

Cook's tip: Try red and yellow peppers and spring onions for a change, with basil to garnish.

Alaska has the cleanest and most natural marine environment of its size on earth. The icy waters around Alaska's 34,000 miles of coastline, its three million lakes and 3,000 rivers provide a perfect and pure habitat for Alaska seafood. Alaska also has very little heavy industry, with strict regulations regarding development. This helps maintain its clean and healthy environment. Careful management of the fisheries ensures the long-term abundance of the seafood species and the continued health of the surrounding eco-system. This means that wild Alaska seafood can be enjoyed by future generations without compromising the

wild ALASKA SEAFOOD

natural

pristine and natural beauty of Alaska. Swimming freely and feeding on a diet of crustaceans and other marine life in their intended habitat means that all Alaska seafood is free from artificial colourings and flavourings. Natural migratory patterns from river to ocean to river give wild Alaska seafood its lean, firm texture valued the world over. The benefits of eating seafood are well known - and the firm, lean texture and superior flavour make wild Alaska seafood the perfect nutritional choice. Alaska seafood is high in protein, vitamins, minerals, and omega 3 oils, which as part of a balanced diet may help to maintain a healthy heart.

wild ALASKA SEAFOOD   77

WILD ALASKA SEAFOOD SUSHI

Serves 4

100g (4oz) sushi rice
2 tbsp rice wine vinegar
$1/2$ tsp caster sugar
$1/2$ tsp salt
4 sheets nori (edible seaweed sheets)
100g (4oz) smoked wild Alaska salmon
1 avocado, peeled, pitted and cut into strips

$1/2$ cucumber, deseeded and cut into fine strips
Juice of $1/2$ lemon
50g (2oz) wild Alaska crab cooked, sliced or flaked
2-3 tbsp wild Alaska salmon caviar (optional)
Pickled ginger, wasabi paste and soy sauce, to serve

Cook the sushi rice according to pack instructions. After it has simmered for 10 minutes, turn off the heat and let it stand for 10 minutes with the lid on. Transfer to a bowl and stir in the rice wine vinegar, sugar and salt.

Making one roll at a time, lay out a single sheet of nori on a sushi-rolling mat. Cover the nori with a thin layer of the cooked sushi rice leaving a 1cm ($1/2$ in) border at the edge farthest away from you. Place strips of smoked salmon along the centre of the rice, horizontally, and position strips of avocado and cucumber on top. Sprinkle with a few drops of lemon juice.

Moisten the border with a little water, and roll up tightly from the front end. The moistened border will stick the roll together. Use a sharp knife to slice the roll into individual pieces. Repeat with the remaining nori sheets.

Shape the remaining sushi rice into small oblongs and top with neat slices of smoked salmon and crab. Top with a little salmon caviar, if desired.

Cover the sushi and keep refrigerated until ready to serve. Serve with pickled ginger, wasabi paste and soy sauce.

Cook's tip: Sprinkle your hands with a little rice wine vinegar to help prevent the sushi rice from sticking to them.

WILD PACIFIC COD IN MISO BROTH WITH UDON NOODLES

Serves 2

4 tsp miso bouillon powder
500ml (18fl oz) water
2 tbsp teriyaki sauce or soy sauce
1 red chilli, deseeded and thinly sliced
4 spring onions, shredded
75g (3oz) mushrooms, thinly sliced
250g (9oz) pack fresh stir-fry vegetables

2 x 150g packs ready-to-use udon (thick) noodles
15g ($^1/_2$ oz) butter
1 tbsp toasted sesame oil
2 x 100-150g (4-6oz) fillets wild Pacific cod, skinned
Sweet chilli sauce, to serve (optional)

Put the miso bouillon powder into a wok or large saucepan and add the water and teriyaki or soy sauce. Bring up to the boil, then reduce the heat and add the chilli, spring onions, mushrooms and stir-fry vegetables. Simmer over a low heat for 5 minutes, add the noodles and cook gently for 5 more minutes.

At the same time, cook the fish. Heat the butter and sesame oil in a frying pan and add the cod fillets, searing them over a high heat on each side. Turn the heat down and cook for a further 5 or 6 minutes. The flesh will be opaque and should flake easily when tested with a fork.

Ladle the noodle mixture into two wide bowls and sit a cod fillet on top of each one. Serve at once with some sweet chilli sauce, if desired.

Cook's tips: Make this dish another time with fillets of wild Alaska salmon. Choose an interesting mix of stir-fry vegetables, with pak choi, peanut shoots and Chinese leaves.

WILD ALASKA HALIBUT SALTIMBOCCA

Serves 4

8 fresh sage leaves
4 x 100-150g (4-6oz) fillets wild Alaska halibut
8 slices Parma Ham
25g (1oz) butter
1 tbsp olive oil

6 tbsp Marsala
4 tbsp vegetable stock
Freshly ground black pepper
Fine green beans, to serve

Place two sage leaves on top of each piece of halibut, season with a little black pepper, then wrap each fish fillet in two slices of Parma Ham.

Heat the butter and olive oil in a large frying pan. Add the Parma-wrapped fillets and cook them over a medium-high heat for 2 minutes on each side.

Pour in the Marsala and add the stock. Turn the heat to low, then simmer gently for about 5 minutes to reduce the liquid, turning the fish fillets once.

Meanwhile, cook the green beans in lightly salted boiling water until just tender - about 4 or 5 minutes.

Serve the fish with the green beans, spooning the reduced sauce over the halibut.

Cook's tip: Buttered new potatoes go brilliantly with this recipe, so put some on to cook before you prepare the fish.

WILD ALASKA BLACK COD WITH ASPARAGUS, CHORIZO & TOMATOES

Serves 4

4 tbsp olive oil
250g (9oz) asparagus spears
4 x 150-200g (6-7oz) fillets wild Alaska black cod
1/2 lemon, juiced

100g (4oz) Spanish chorizo sausage, sliced
4 small bunches cherry tomatoes on the vine
Freshly ground black pepper

Preheat a char-grill pan or the grill. Use 1 or 2 tablespoons of the olive oil to brush over the asparagus spears. Char-grill or grill them for about 5 or 6 minutes, turning often, until cooked.

Meanwhile, heat the remaining olive oil in a frying pan and add the fillets of black cod, cooking them over a medium heat for about 6 to 8 minutes. Add the slices of chorizo and cook for 3 or 4 more minutes. Check that the fish is cooked - the flesh should be opaque and flake easily when tested with a fork. If necessary, cook for a little longer.

Lightly cook the vine tomato bunches, either in the char-grill pan or under the grill. They will only need a couple of minutes.

Serve the black cod with the asparagus, chorizo and tomatoes, sprinkled with freshly ground black pepper.

Cook's tip: Remember that thick fillets of black cod will take a little longer to cook.

WILD ALASKA CRAB MINI POPPADOMS

Look out for bite-sized mini poppadoms - they're brilliant for this clever nibble. Just mix some cooked **flaked wild Alaska crab** with a little **mayonnaise** or natural yoghurt. Season with **freshly ground black pepper**, some **finely grated lime or lemon zest** and a squeeze of **lime or lemon juice**, then add a little finely chopped **red or green chilli**, a couple of finely chopped **spring onions** and some chopped **fresh coriander**. Pile onto the **mini poppadoms** and garnish with coriander leaves, if you wish.

SMOKED WILD ALASKA SALMON, MINI SANDWICHES

Serve these cute sandwiches at a party or with pre-dinner drinks. Just spread medium slices of **buttered brown and white bread** with **cream cheese** - flavoured with herbs, if you like. Top with pieces of **smoked wild Alaska salmon** and thinly sliced **cucumber**. Sprinkle with a little lemon juice or white wine vinegar, then season with **freshly ground black pepper**. Sandwich together with buttered bread, then stamp into circles with a small biscuit cutter, or slice into squares, removing the crusts.

POACHED WILD ALASKA SALMON PATE

Ever wondered what to serve for a tasty, stylish canapé? Then try these little croustades. First, poach a 200g (7oz) **wild Alaska salmon fillet** in simmering stock for 6 to 8 minutes, until the flesh is opaque and flakes easily. Drain and let it cool, then flake with a fork. Add 2 tbsp of **Greek-style natural yoghurt**, 2 tbsp of **mayonnaise**, a squeeze of **lemon juice** and a little finely chopped **fresh dill**. Season, then spoon into mini croustades and serve, garnished with finely chopped **red and yellow peppers** and tiny sprigs of dill.

WILD ALASKA SALMON TERIYAKI WITH WASABI DIP

Take some small bamboo skewers and soak them in hot water for 10 minutes, then thread chunks of skinless **wild Alaska salmon fillet** onto them. Lay them in a shallow dish and spoon **teriyaki marinade** over them - you'll need about 100ml (3 $^1/_2$ fl oz). Leave them to marinate for at least half an hour, covered and chilled. Grill for 3 or 4 minutes, turning often. Serve with a dip made from 150g (5oz) **crème fraiche** or Greek-style natural yoghurt mixed with 3 or 4 tsp of **wasabi paste** or horseradish sauce.

WILD ALASKA CRAB LINGUINE WITH CAPERS & BASIL

Serves 4

400g (14oz) linguine or spaghetti
25g (1oz) butter
1 red chilli, deseeded and thinly sliced
200g (7oz) soft cheese (plain or
with herbs and garlic)
3 tbsp milk

350g (12oz) wild Alaska crab meat, cooked and
flaked
2-3 tbsp capers, drained
4 tbsp Parmesan cheese, finely grated
Salt and freshly ground black pepper
Basil leaves, to garnish

Cook the linguine or spaghetti in plenty of lightly salted boiling water for 6 to 8 minutes until just tender, or follow the pack instructions.

Meanwhile, melt the butter and gently fry the chilli until softened for about 2 minutes. Add the soft cheese and milk. Heat gently, stirring constantly with a small whisk or wooden spoon, until the cheese has melted and the sauce is smooth. Remove from the heat and stir occasionally.

Drain the cooked pasta, and return it to the saucepan. Add the crab, capers and cheese sauce. Heat for a few moments, stirring gently. Season with freshly ground black pepper, then share between four warm plates or bowls.

Cook's tip: Serve at once, scattered with the Parmesan cheese and basil leaves

WILD ALASKA POLLOCK SUPPER, MEXICAN-STYLE

Serves 4

350g (12oz) wild Alaska pollock fillet, thawed if frozen
2 tbsp olive oil
1 onion, finely chopped
1 large garlic clove, crushed
2 green chillies, deseeded and finely chopped
300ml ($^1/_2$ pt) passata
1 x 215g can re-fried beans

Salt and freshly ground black pepper
8 soft flour tortillas
75g (3oz) Cheddar cheese, grated
1 large ripe avocado
1 lime, juiced
Fresh soured cream, to serve
Coriander sprigs and chopped red onion to garnish (optional)

Pat the fish fillets dry with kitchen paper, then cut them into large chunks.

Preheat the oven to 190°C / fan oven 170°C / Gas Mark 5. Grease a large oblong baking dish with a little olive oil.

Heat the remaining olive oil in a frying pan and gently fry the onion, garlic and chillies for 3 or 4 minutes, until softened. Stir in the passata, re-fried beans and chunks of fish. Season with salt and pepper and cook gently for 2 minutes.

Lay the tortillas on a work surface and share the fish mixture between them. Roll them up and place in the baking dish, seam side down. Sprinkle the grated cheese over the top. Bake for 20-25 minutes until piping hot.

While the tortillas are baking, make the guacamole by mashing the avocado and mixing it with the lime juice.

Serve the baked tortillas with the guacamole and sour cream. Garnish with fresh coriander and chopped red onion, if you like.

Cook's tip: Wild Alaska pollock is an economical fish that tastes good in spicy recipes, like this Mexican inspired dish.

WARM WILD ALASKA SALMON, FENNEL AND TOMATO SALAD

Serves 4

25g (1oz) butter
6 tbsp olive oil
450g (1lb) wild Alaska salmon fillet
100g (4oz) frozen broad beans
3 tbsp red wine vinegar
1 tsp Dijon mustard

Salt and freshly ground black pepper
1 bulb fennel, very thinly sliced
4 beef tomatoes, sliced
4 tbsp capers, rinsed
2 sprigs fresh dill

Melt the butter in a frying pan and add a few drops of the olive oil. Add the salmon fillets and cook them over a medium-high heat for 3 or 4 minutes on each side. Remove from the pan and leave them to cool.

Cook the broad beans in boiling, lightly salted water for 3 or 4 minutes. Rinse with cold water, then shell the beans, removing their thicker outer coating to reveal the bright, tender green beans.

In a large bowl, mix the remaining olive oil with the vinegar and mustard. Season with a pinch of salt and ground black pepper. Add the fennel, tomatoes, broad beans and capers.

Break up the salmon into large chunks, and then add them to the salad bowl, tossing gently to mix. Share between four serving plates, spooning any remaining dressing over them. Snip the fresh dill over the top, then serve.

Cook's tip: Use fresh broad beans when they are in season, or try frozen soya beans as an alternative.

WILD ALASKA POLLOCK WITH POTTED PRAWNS

Serves 4

225g (8oz) wild Alaska pollock fillet,
thawed if frozen
2 spring onions, very finely chopped
2 tbsp fresh parsley, chopped
2 tsp lemon juice
225g (8oz) small cooked peeled prawns,
thawed if frozen

50g (2oz) fresh white breadcrumbs
Freshly ground black pepper
100g (4oz) butter, melted
Brown bread and butter or toast, to serve

Put the fish fillets into a frying pan and cover with water. Heat and simmer gently for 6 to 8 minutes, or until the fish is opaque and the flesh flakes easily when tested with a fork. Drain thoroughly, discarding the cooking liquid. Cool, and flake with a fork.

Mix the flaked fish with the spring onions, parsley, lemon juice, prawns and breadcrumbs. Season with black pepper. Add most of the melted butter, stir well, and transfer the mixture to four ramekin dishes or one large pot. Pour the reserved butter over the surface. Chill until ready to serve.

Enjoy with brown bread and butter or toast triangles.

Cook's tip: Swap the pollock for wild Alaska salmon, halibut or Pacific cod for a different taste.

WILD ALASKA SALMON PENNE WITH GREEN BEANS AND VINAIGRETTE

Serves 4

350g (12oz) penne (or other pasta shapes)
15g (¹/₂ oz) butter
4 tbsp olive oil
350g (12oz) wild Alaska salmon fillet, skinned
150g (6oz) fine green beans, trimmed and halved

Finely grated zest and juice of 1 lemon
1 tbsp fresh lemon thyme leaves
Salt and freshly ground black pepper
Lemon wedges and sprigs of lemon thyme, to garnish

Cook the pasta in plenty of lightly salted boiling water for about 10 minutes, or according to pack instructions.

Meanwhile, heat the butter with 1 tablespoon of the olive oil in a frying pan. Add the salmon fillet and cook for 5 or 6 minutes, turning once. At the same time, cook the green beans in lightly salted boiling water for 3 or 4 minutes, and drain them thoroughly.

Drain the cooked pasta, reserving 2 tablespoons of the cooking liquid, then return both to the saucepan. Add the green beans, lemon zest and juice, thyme leaves and remaining olive oil.

Break the salmon fillet into chunks and add them to the pan. Stir everything together gently over a medium heat for 1 or 2 minutes. Season to taste, then serve, garnished with lemon wedges and thyme sprigs.

Cook's tip: Sprinkle a few capers over the finished dish, if you like them.